The Power of Cold

The Power of Cold

How to Embrace the Cold
and Change Your Life

NÍALL Ó MURCHÚ

Hardie Grant

BOOKS

Contents

CHAPTER 3: TEACHINGS OF
THE COLD

A Warning
of Sorts

The cold is a powerful force. It must be respected at all times. We should never try to force anything in the cold. We should never try to fight it. We must always use our common sense and be safe.

This book will take us along a path that shows us how to use the cold as a force for good in our lives.

If you hate the cold, but know it could help you, then this path will provide you with the guidance and support you need. If you already swim in the sea, take cold showers or jump into ice baths, then this path will help you get more from your efforts. It will take you into the depths of the cold; where you can learn a lot about yourself. It will open up a path to mastery.

You don't have to live beside the sea to get great benefits from the cold (or this book). You don't need a DryRobe either. No matter where you live, you can learn to use the cold to enrich your days.

All you have to do is follow the path.

Warning: as you move along the path, you may even begin to love the cold. You've been warned.

You, Me and the Cold

You and I have shared a special journey; before we entered the world, we were cradled in the comfort of the womb. It was a place of safety and protection, where we were nurtured and sustained – despite what was happening in the outside world, we were secure in warmth. It may have been dark, but we were surrounded and reassured by the beating of our mother's heart and her breathing provided us with life. Everyone has experienced this sense of safety at some point.

Then things suddenly changed and we were pushed into a new world. The noises and light changed, and there was sudden cold. Our first gasp of breath was triggered by the shock of the cold on our skin. Our lungs sprang to life, pumping and pushing for the first time. The cold ignited life within us. From that moment on, our breathing and the cold were intimately connected. It was the cold that gave us our first breath and our first experience of life.

Many people, from that moment on, have spent the rest of their lives trying to avoid the cold. They have grown to hate it. They would do anything to avoid it. But perhaps there is a deep part of us that was prepared for the shock of the cold – a part that knows that the cold is a fundamental part of life?

Maybe we need the cold to feel whole again?

Maybe the cold can teach us how to breathe again?

Maybe it can help us come alive again?

Maybe it can teach us to find calm in the chaos again?

This book is about finding that path back down into the cold. It's about learning to use the cold as a force for good in our lives. It's about learning to use it to enrich our days.

WHY BOTHER GETTING INTO THE COLD?

Jamie is a fireman and a big handsome one at that. I met him at one of my retreats in the west of Ireland. Sadly, his family had gone through an unfathomable tragedy and Jamie needed a way to deal with the trauma, anger and pain of what had happened. This is what he told me about the cold:

'After a shocking family tragedy, I felt everything was just too much. I felt life was just relentless. Everything was just moving too fast. My anxiety levels were sky high. I felt anger and sadness and I just needed something to calm my mind and slow everything down, so I could hear my own self. And I found my voice in the cold.'

My alarm usually goes off at 5 a.m. I desperately scramble around for it in the dark, trying to turn it off before it wakes everyone. It's an old-school travel clock and the sound it makes is ear-splitting. But, it works. It wakes me up.

When I get up, I ask myself: 'How do I feel?' Most days, now, my body feels light and loose. I usually feel refreshed after a night's sleep with good levels of energy. Most importantly, my mind feels open and calm and ready to focus on what's next. Most days.

But, before I started getting into the cold, things were very different. I would wake up feeling rusty and stiff. I found it hard to lift my head off the pillow: I would wake up tired (often even exhausted), which is a hard way to start the day. My mind would also be cluttered with all the things I had to do and people I had to see. Have you ever felt like that?

Everything started to change once I got into the cold.

After a few days of cold showers, things were starting to shift. At the time, my four children were all very young and the mornings in our house were unpleasant. To get the four children up, teeth brushed, uniforms on, breakfast eaten and heading in the right direction was stressful and difficult. By the time I was on my bike, on the way to work, I was wrecked. But, a few days after starting the cold showers, things were changing.

My wife, Josie, has a beautiful singing voice and she was singing to the children in the kitchen one morning. It was three days after we started the cold showers. We were all playing and laughing. It felt light and cheerful. No stress. No difficulty. I had to stop at one point and ask myself: 'What the hell is going on here?'

The answer lay in the cold.

When we get into the cold our hormones can balance, changing our mood. It helps us feel more alert, more alive, energised and happy. It can reduce feelings of stress and anxiety. We feel different after the cold. We feel more like ourselves. We feel balanced. We feel triumphant; it's like a victory for us every time we do it and that is what Josie and I were feeling from the cold showers. But it wasn't just Josie and I who were discovering the benefits of the cold; science started to pay attention too.

Professor Giovanna Mallucci, who runs the UK Dementia Research Institute's Centre at the University of Cambridge, found that the cold may protect the brain from degenerative diseases like dementia. The British Medical Journal found that the cold could help with anxiety and depression.

So, Josie and I continued to explore the cold a little more. Three weeks after we had started the cold showers, things were different: we didn't feel as tired. We were more patient with the children and each other. We felt stronger and braver. It was December, and the winter had deepened. Josie said: 'Why don't we go to Seapoint for a swim in the sea?'

I know swimming in the sea is popular now, but all those years ago it was not. Back then, only a few people were getting into the sea and they were often considered unhinged! But, with our new-found energy and bravery, we decided to give it a go.

If you are looking out to sea, at Seapoint in Monkstown, Dublin, there is a cement ramp on the left-hand side that runs down into the sea. Josie had been in the freezing water and was walking up that ramp out of the sea. She felt so alive, so powerful and strong that she shouted over to me: 'I feel like I can lift up our car!' Two things you need to know at this point: one – Josie is quite a small person and doesn't lift too many heavy objects. Two – our car is a giant 7-seater. So, again, I asked myself: 'What the hell is going on here?' Three weeks ago we could hardly lift our heads off the pillow and now Josie is talking about lifting our car around South County Dublin!

Anyone who has been in the cold knows that feeling afterwards. We feel invincible and uplifted. The cold changes us.

But, it goes deeper than that. The cold can improve our immunity, which makes us healthier (obviously) but also gives us a greater sense of freedom. We're not as afraid of getting sick. Our circulation can get better, pumping blood and nutrients to parts of our body that may not have been getting enough beforehand. That helps us feel more alive. Our recovery from injury or sickness or stress can improve. The cold can decrease inflammation, which is the cause of many of our health problems, and it can reduce pain. Josie was feeling all of that as she emerged from the water in Monkstown. So, we kept going.

But, it wasn't only us feeling the benefits. Josie and I met Lisa at the sea. Lisa had suffered from chronic illness most of her life. This is what she told me:

'When you're so sick, your own body doesn't feel like home any more. During high pain days I've frequently found myself muttering, "I want to go home." As soon as I'm in the cold water and it's supporting my body, reducing the pain, and allowing my chest to breathe better, I'm home.'

Inspired by all these benefits, Josie and I continued along the path of the cold. Three months after we had started, I was transformed. Before I started getting into the cold, I woke up feeling tired. Now, I feel refreshed. Before, I woke up feeling rusty and stiff. Now, I feel light and loose. I used to wake up and my mind was cluttered. Now, my mind feels clear and peaceful. Most of the time.

But, there was more than that. If I could gather up all the benefits I felt, Josie felt, and the ripple effect it had on our family, friends and community, it would be this: it gave Josie and I the strength and bravery to make some big decisions. I chose to leave my old job and start a new business with Josie, following this path of the cold and trying to help as many people as we could along the way. That is the reason this book is in your hands right now.

There is a path down into the cold that everyone can follow, and when we do, it can transform us. I asked Nicole, a working mother of three teenagers who is often in the sea, why should we bother getting into the cold?

'The cold makes us feel alive, powerful, connected, present, exhilarated, energised and calm. It's a reset. It blows my mind every time.'

The path into the cold can truly transform us. It can help us let go of fear and worry. It can help us feel alive again. It can help us become more loving and open. It can help us find a sense of calm and control despite the chaos and stress we might face. I have felt it. Millions of other people have felt it. The cold can transform us, but it begins in chaos.

'In the bitterness
of the cold,

one finds the
sweetness of true
warmth.'

RUMI
PERSIAN POET AND SUFI MYSTIC

Chapter 1

The Path

Into the Chaos

The path into the cold is a path into chaos, fear and uncertainty – just like our first moments of life, when the cold shocks us into taking our very first breath. But it's also a path to finding control and calm, despite all that pressure and struggle. The cold can teach us how to live, and live well, despite stress and uncertainty trying to push us out of balance. The cold, like water, can be soft and healing but it can also be brutal and powerful. That's what we must embrace; that the cold can become a force for good in our lives.

But, first comes the chaos.

Picture the scene: a wide open beach, with salt in the air and circling seagulls high in the sky. Waves crash on the shore and a group of children leave their parents behind and sprint down into the water. You can hear their shrieks and screams as they leap in and out of the waves, dealing with the sharp coldness of the water. There is shock. There is joy. There is a lightness as they find their way into the cold.

For many adults, the path into the cold is similar: there might be screams and shrieks. There might be a sense of joy. But, more likely, there will be a sense of fear, shock, doubt and tenseness beforehand. The path into the cold is a difficult one. So, why take those steps into the surf?

At the beginning, there is a decision to be made: Why are we doing it? What do we want to get from the experience?

Here are my suggestions:
We learn to use the cold as a force for good in our lives.
We learn to use the cold as a way to enrich our lives.
We learn to use the cold to find control and calm in the chaos.

So, that is the first step: to set a clear intention.

It's important that we are clear about this because the cold will test us. It will test our resolve. It will test our spirit. It will shock us. It will confuse us. It will make us question why we are doing this.

There have been many moments along the path when I have questioned why I am doing this. The one that jumps to mind immediately was a dark morning before dawn in a forest, high up in the mountains, on an expedition, surrounded by icy and snowy peaks. I was stumbling down the forest path in the dark (the sun hadn't yet crept over the mountaintops) down to a river of ice. It was about -10°C. I was there to cut a large hole in the ice so my group could get into the river later in the day. With an axe held high on my shoulder, with my breath freezing in the air in front of me, I questioned what I was doing. 'What the hell am I doing here?' I thought. I reached the river and it was eerily silent. Instead of a rushing river, it was frozen over. I sat down on my bum and began to scoot over the rocks towards the river's edge. The rocks were encased in ice. 'Why am I doing this?' I asked myself.

These moments are important: they force us to examine our motives deeply (and truthfully).

I was doing this because learning how to deal with the chaos of the cold had transformed me. The cold had become a force for good in my life. I wanted other people to experience that too. That was why I was slipping and tripping over the icy rocks. This was in my mind as I began hacking away at the ice with the axe. It was slow work, but eventually a hole in the ice began to appear. The sun was rising. It was glittering on the broken shards of ice. I could see the freezing water rushing under the ice. It was time to get in.

Enter the chaos. Just like those first few moments of life, exposed to the shock of the cold.

The path into the cold begins by removing layers. Yes, we remove layers of clothes. In another sense, we are removing layers of protection. We are removing layers of comfort and embracing the discomfort that follows. We are removing layers of façade and masks, too. We have to embrace our vulnerabilities because the cold gives them nowhere to hide. They are now on display.

So, there I was, nowhere to hide, standing there in my swimming togs.

I had taken off my clothes and the icy wind was beginning to bite into my exposed skin. I looked down and saw a brown leaf frozen in the ice under my bare foot. The journey into the depths had begun. I started to control my breathing and to control the fear rising in my chest.

In the coming pages, you will learn how to do that as well.

Dark, conflicting thoughts jumped up through my mind as I slid towards the hole in the ice. My mind was screaming to go back. But, my breathing started to control that too.

In the coming pages, you will learn how to do that as well.

Ice can be as sharp as broken glass. So, I had to be careful as I lowered myself into the water. I quickly forgot about everything else as the vice-grip of the cold began to squeeze. Immediately, my fingers and toes exploded with pain, immediately my mind was awash with a frenzy of thoughts – mostly 'Get the ***k out!' In that moment, my body made an infinite number of calculations and adjustments, constricting kilometres of blood vessels, releasing a heady mix of chemicals into my blood, trying to find a way to survive.

The chaos was underway.

What do we do, then, when we're fully immersed in an emergency? When our heart is pounding through our chest? When we're feeling extreme stress? We can feel all of that in the cold. But lots of other difficult circumstances bring about those feelings too: pressure in work can do it. Pressure at home can do it. Anxious thoughts can do it. Chaos comes in many forms.

The path into the cold begins with chaos. Then comes the control.

Control

It was getting intense. He was standing right in front of me, staring straight into my eyes. He was big: fists clenched, looking like he was ready to fight. But of course he wasn't. My teenage son and I were arguing over a mountain bike. It was getting heated. We were standing in the front room of our home in Dublin, the sunshine streaming in through the window. I felt I had been a good parent when my children were small. But, as they became teenagers, I had to learn how to be a parent again. It was a work in progress. The argument was going around in illogical circles. We were getting more frustrated as we went. Within me, a mixture of anger, pain and love was bubbling up. I had to control my reactions. I wanted to sort it all out without things flaring up.

The cold had taught me how to control my breath despite its pressure. It had taught me to find my breath in among the chaos and to focus on slow exhales. The cold had taught me that once I had my breathing under control, I had myself under control. Then, I could make the right decision.

In life, as with the cold, chaos and suffering finds us. But, when we learn to focus on our breath, that chaos can be transformed into a sense of control. Then we have a choice: we don't just react to a situation. Instead, there is a little bit of space between the situation happening and our reaction to it. We have a choice in that moment: how do we want to react?

That is what the cold had taught me. That is what it can teach you too.

Families can be very difficult, especially when raising a house full of teenagers. There is a dance between control and surrender. This isn't just for parents. Our lives are dominated by this need to balance control and surrender. It has dominated the minds of philosophers and seekers of the truth since the beginning of time:

'Letting go, far from being disempowering, is empowering,' Krishna said in *The Bhagavad Gita*.

And it's at the heart of our experience in the cold: surrender and control.

Control can come in many forms. When it's light, control can help us react to a situation in a way we want to. The cold teaches us that in a difficult situation we have a choice: with practice we can control how we feel and how we think and how we react to that pressure. When it's dark and heavy, control can be an extension of fear. It can reach out into our thoughts and actions: we want things to happen in a certain way, in a fixed way, and we can feel threatened and unsafe when the situation doesn't unfold like we want it to.

What's the opposite of this control? Surrender.

Surrender is a practice that is central to nearly all religious traditions. Can we let go of fear and anger (if it would be advantageous to do so)? Can we let go, and surrender, unhelpful feelings (or thoughts) as they arise in us? Can we let go of worry? Can we let go of fear? Can we accept what is happening?

Control and surrender: sometimes we get the balance right and sometimes we don't. That is why we need the cold. That leads us back to the story of the frozen river ...

As I lowered myself into the water below the thick ice, my body flashed into fight-or-flight mode. The intensity of the cold was pushing my body into a state of emergency: my mind had exploded in chaos. But then all the training kicked in: I was able to find my breath in among all the chaos. I was able to focus on my breathing. I was able to begin to work on breathing out slowly and calmly. It didn't happen straight away. But I knew that if I kept working on those exhales, the control would come.

Five, six, seven exhales into the experience and I started to feel like I was gaining control of my breath. I stayed with those exhales; they became calmer, slower and more in control. Then, it happened, my vagus nerve kicked in. I could feel my heart rate slow down. I could feel my body soften. My breathing was in control and slowing down. I could look around and marvel at the beauty of the thick ice glistening in the rising sun. It was beautiful. It felt great.

I had found a sense of control in the cold. You'll learn how to do this too.

As you read through this book, as you follow this path, you'll be able to find that sense of control as well. Not only in the cold, but in all types of pressure. We will learn to do this step by step. Don't worry: the path doesn't lead into an ice bath (although it could). You will move at your own pace. You will find a cold practice that works for you. The most important thing is that we learn how to find a sense of control in the chaos. When we do, everything changes. That is what the cold can teach us.

But, what happens after the control?

Well, that is where the deepest benefits are. When we have control of our breathing, then we can slow it down. We can soften our body despite the pressure. We can feel a deep sense of calm no matter what is happening. We can let go of whatever tension or stress we have been carrying. We can surrender to what is happening. We can accept things as they unfold. We can follow our breath down this path to a place where we feel calm and peaceful, where we can fall in love with everything.

That is what the cold can teach us. That is where the path takes us next.

'The cold can be a
source of

inspiration,
invigoration, and
creativity.'

HENRY DAVID THOREAU
AMERICAN WRITER AND PHILOSOPHER

Calm

After the chaos and shock of the cold, comes a sense of control. After the control, comes a sense of deepening calm. But what does that feel like?

Firstly, our body begins to soften as it lets go of whatever tension it might be holding. Secondly, our breathing is slow and steady. We feel safe and assured. Our minds feel strong and open. We feel at peace. We feel we can handle whatever comes next. We can observe our thoughts and decide to follow them or not. When we feel like this, we can let go of stress and anxiety. When we feel like this, we can let go of worry and fear. When we feel like this, we can let go of thoughts or feelings we might be struggling with.

When we are down in this part of the nervous system (parasympathetic) we feel peaceful and the body can begin to restore and heal itself. Sounds great, right? But how do we get there? How can we learn to do all that?

The cold can teach us.

All we have to do is follow the path down into its depths. That is what you will do over the coming pages. I will plot a path for you to learn how to use the cold to find calm despite the pressure. That will enrich your life. As it has mine and that of countless other people.

'Yeah, but does it take us 40 years of meditating in a zen monastery? I have a job and lots of things to do!' I hear you say.

No, the path from chaos to control to calmness can be learned quickly and even by people who hate the cold.

But, before we start, I want to describe to you what it actually feels like. So, let's go back to my story about getting into the frozen river. I'm neck-deep in ice: once I had gotten control of my breath in the freezing river, everything began to change. I was no longer frightened. I was no longer panicking. I was no longer in emergency mode. Of course, I could feel the pressure of the cold, but my breathing was rhythmic and steady.

Then, it began: I began to slow down my breathing a little bit. My breathing steadied. The pressure in my breathing had lessened and that gave me more control over it. I felt I was getting a hold of my feelings too. That allowed me to slow down. That started to calm me down. My breathing became soft and light.

I became aware that my body was tense under the water - my shoulders were like balls of stress. So, on my next exhale, I allowed them to soften. I noticed my fists and feet were balled-up tightly like I was ready to fight. On my next exhale, I softened those parts of my body. I became aware that my body was softening now despite the pressure of the cold.

I thought: 'If I can find this sense of relaxation and comfort down here in the cold, I can find it anywhere, under any pressure.' This is what you will learn as you follow this path. You will learn to find a sense of calm in times of pressure, stress and struggle.

There was a moment then, which I have felt many times since (and that many people in the cold have felt too), that I can only describe like this:

I fell in love with everything. I fell in love with the cold. I fell in love with the struggle. I fell in love with the feeling of calm. I fell in love with all the trees around. I fell in love with the rising sun. I fell in love with everything.

I also felt I could have stayed there forever. This was the peak.

You will also feel this. Once you have settled into your breathing, you will feel calm and safe despite the constant pressure (and pain) of the cold. At that point, we feel we can stay in the cold for ages. But, here, hidden among these feelings of love and triumph, is danger.

Danger?

Yes, if we want the cold to be a force for good in our lives – an enriching experience – then, less is more. When we feel this peak of calm, of peace, of tranquillity, that is enough: we are getting all the benefits we have talked about before. When we have reached this peak, and we get out, we carry all those feelings of power, of warmth or of strength with us for the rest of the day. When we go to the peak, to the moment we fall in love with everything, to when we feel we can stay in forever, that is when we get out.

We're in the cold for a good time, not a long time.

That, of course, is if our intention is for the cold to be a force for good in our lives. Of course, if a person's intention in the cold is different, then their approach will be different. If they want to explore what is beyond the peak, for example. Or, maybe they are training for a swimming race in the sea. That is different. They will want to stay longer than the peak. But, if we want the cold to be a force for good in our lives, then we must listen to our bodies, never force and look for that peak. That is enough.

How do we know we have reached the peak? We listen to our breath.

Here's how: at first, we experience chaos and shock in the cold. Then, we find our breath within that chaos. We focus on bringing our breath under control, putting our attention on long, slow exhales. We rhythmically work on our exhales until they begin to come fully under our control.

When our exhales are under our control, we begin to slow them down. When they start to slow, we will begin to feel calm. We stay focused on those exhales as we become peaceful and calm. We settle into these feelings of solace, we soften our body, letting go of any tension or stress or struggle we might be holding. We can leave all of that behind us in the cold.

Now, let's begin...

Chapter 2

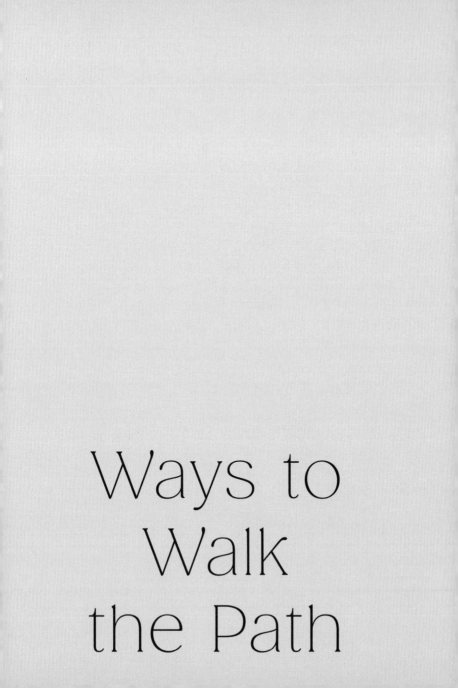

Ways to
Walk
the Path

Cold Hands

What do you think of when you imagine a marijuana grower? I had one in my group on a retreat and he had colourful tattoos running down both arms, taught yoga and lived in California. He was relaxed (as you'd expect) and interesting. His brand of marijuana was well-known in California. We chatted regularly on our adventures throughout the retreat. I enjoyed his company.

As we were coming to the end of the retreat, I set the group one of their final tasks: training their hands in the cold. There's a few important reasons we do this: when approached with respect (see the section *Listen to Your Body*), it can improve the circulation in our hands, build mental resilience, help us deal better with stress, and much more. On that day, in the forest, my group and I stood in a circle and I warned them:

'Putting our hands in the cold can be very difficult, painful even. Our body knows we can just pull our hands back out of the water; our nervous system is sending messages to our brains to get them out of there. So, this can get uncomfortable very fast. But, take your time, feel the sensations in your hands, use your breathing, especially your exhale to take control of your breath. Listen to your body and don't push, just take your hands out when you're ready.'

I don't think they really believed me. They had been in the cold repeatedly over the previous days and had gained a lot of experience. So, they were a little dismissive. We made our way to the edge of the little stream. It was a beautiful spot: ancient trees reaching out over our heads and a slow, meandering stream running near our feet. The water in the stream was cold. They crouched down by the water and put their hands in.

I was standing close by, watching their reactions. The nearest person to me was the laid-back marijuana grower. He was crouched down, hands in the water. He had turned to me suddenly, staring at me intensely. He shouted across the water at me: 'You bastard!' He was shocked by his reaction (and the sensations in his hands). I wasn't. There was no malice in what he said. He was laughing and shaking his hands dry as he stood up. He hadn't expected the intensity of the feeling. He had to lash out at someone: might as well be me! We had a good laugh about his unexpected reaction.

Within the next hour or so, you'll probably wash your hands: maybe you'll go to the toilet, maybe you'll be preparing food or you'll just feel like washing your hands. Whatever the reason, wash your hands in your usual way with warm water. Gently place your attention on your hands as you do this – enjoy the feeling of that hot water on your skin. Now, turn the tap to cold, let it run for a moment, and put your hands under the cold water. Notice how your hands feel. Notice how your breath changes. Notice where your thoughts run to. Over the next 24 hours, whenever you wash your hands, finish with a dash of cold. As the day goes on, notice how you feel as you prepare to wash your hands. What thoughts are arising in your mind? How are you feeling as you approach the sink? This is about watching our reactions to the cold.

This is our first step to building a new relationship with the cold.

Maybe you already swim in a local lake every day. So this task might seem easy to you. But it isn't about endurance; this task is about beginning to really feel the sensation of cold on the body, examining those sensations, giving them your attention, trying to understand them more. This is the first step in changing how our body understands the cold.

If this is the first time you have ever done anything like this, then take your time. Like I said, this isn't an endurance test. It isn't a form of self-imposed torture either. This is helping us become familiar with the shock of the cold. This is helping us become aware of our own reactions to the cold. This is about building a new relationship with the cold. It is also a great way to change our mood immediately.

When we put our hands in the cold it demands our full attention. For a few moments, all we are thinking about are the sensations in our hands. Everything else is forgotten about. So, in that way, it's like a quick and immediate form of meditation. Also, in those moments, the cold is testing us. We feel a spike in energy as our body prepares to run or fight for its life. Again, this changes our internal state quickly and without much thought. We're also grateful when we take our hands out, appreciating the room temperature a little more!

Just like my friend the marijuana grower – if you want to scream and curse at me too, that's okay!

Training Your Hands

For the next 24 hours, wash your hands as usual with warm water. Then, at the end, turn the tap to really cold and allow the water to run over your hands. Bring your full attention to how your hands feel. How is your body reacting to the cold water? How do your fingers feel? Observe how you feel, how your breathing changes and where your thoughts run to.

Close your eyes for a moment and give the feeling of the cold a colour. What colour is it?

What thoughts are running through your mind? When you've had enough, take your hands out of the cold water and place your attention fully on them again. How does the skin feel? What colour are they? What emotions do you feel? Remember: this isn't an endurance test; use your common sense. Less is more in the cold.

Barefoot

Out the window, frosty fields stretched to the horizon and the wild Atlantic. The sun was bright but the air temperature was freezing; unusually cold for Ireland, even out here on the west coast. The country had been blanketed in snow and ice for a few days. Everything had come to a standstill. My beloved country is not used to the cold and a few centimetres of snow brings everything to a halt.

But I was happy as I wrote these words. I was sitting upstairs in a warm, cosy house overlooking the sea. I was at the beautiful Cliffs of Moher Retreat in County Clare. Despite the weather, everyone who had booked into our retreat showed up. We'd been jumping in and out of ice baths, hot tubs, saunas and snow all day, having great fun. But we were also learning how powerful the cold is, learning to respect it, learning never to force it, but to surrender to its strength, using it as a force for good in our lives.

One thing struck me throughout the whole experience: most of us have to confront the cold at different times of the year. It's often unavoidable. We can either recoil from or hate it and always try to insulate ourselves from it. Or, we can learn to accept it, learn to harness its power to warm ourselves up (more on this in a moment) and embrace it. Over time, we begin to understand the cold differently. Eventually, we crave it. We might even grow to love it.

But, now, let's take it one step at a time. That step is important. Especially when that step is barefoot.

When we step out of our home in our bare feet and walk on the ground, everything changes. It doesn't matter where you are. You could be stepping across the sand on a secluded beach. You could be stepping across the grass in your back garden. You could be stepping across cold concrete. You could be stepping gingerly across gravel. You could be stepping across your cold kitchen floor.

It doesn't matter.

All we have to do is take off our shoes and socks and put our feet on the ground. Feel the surface beneath our feet. Allow our feet to sink into it. Feel the temperature. Feel the texture. Feel how your body reacts to it.

For some people, putting their bare feet on the earth can be an intense experience. Especially when it's cold. Especially when their feet are normally encased in restrictive shoes all the time. But it's an important step along the path of understanding the cold, and ourselves, more deeply.

There are many thousands of nerve endings in the soles of our feet, travelling from there up into our bodies. So, we feel a lot of different sensations when we walk in our bare feet. When I walk on frost or snow, I can feel discomfort in my stomach and even my head sometimes. So, as ever, we must approach the cold respectfully. Less is more in the cold.

So, step out into the rain, into the sunshine, into the frost (and everything in between) and see how it feels.

What I realised, as I sat looking out at the Atlantic at the Cliffs of Moher Retreat, is this: our experience of the cold (and warmth) is relative. It's relative (or to put it another way, it is dependent on) our mood, our levels of stress, our tolerance of the cold, the temperature we feel, and many more things. What I am trying to say is that how we perceive the cold can change as we change. Each morning as I woke before dawn at the retreat, I got out of the nice warm bed and I stumbled downstairs in the dark. The house seemed cold in comparison to the lovely bed I had just gotten out of. I looked outside into the frosty darkness and it looked very cold. But I wanted to test my new understanding. So I opened the door and was immediately shocked by the rush of bracing wild Atlantic air. I took a deep breath and stepped outside onto the Liscannor stone path. The stone was slick with frost and I immediately felt the cold under my feet. I found my breath and started breathing slowly and calmly. The cold felt like electricity running up through my body. It felt sharp. It felt thrilling.

I didn't need much. So, after a short time, I walked back into the house. Just like that: the house felt warm. It felt comfortable and welcoming. While just a few minutes before it was cold and uninviting. I was delighted to be back inside.

By stepping outside, by walking barefoot, my body had to adjust to its new circumstances. It had to adapt. It had to find a way to deal with the cold. It had to find a way to survive, and it did. It changed. It did what we do best: adapt to difficult situations. Thankfully, I didn't have to stay out there very long. Then, when I got back inside, everything was different. The temperature inside felt mellow and warm. Of course, the temperature in the house hadn't changed, but my perception of it had. My feet began to feel warm too, as the blood vessels started to open again and the blood flowed merrily to my extremities.

By embracing the cold, by feeling it underfoot, my body began to adapt to it. So, here was the lesson for me and you: a little dose of cold, especially with our feet, can ignite our bodies into action, finding the spark and heat we need to survive and thrive.

The owner of the Cliffs of Moher Retreat, Michelle, was also a great advocate of the cold. During our time there, she led us on a barefoot walk around the land. As well as the cold, the different textures of the ground – sometimes muddy, sometimes stony, sometimes soft – tested our ability to focus despite the pressure.

And I can tell you, we most definitely cherished the warm room when we made it back inside!

'I've learned that plunging into icy water can bring not just a thrill, and peace to the soul,

but an almost existential
feeling of mental and
physical clarity.'

SUSAN CASEY
AUTHOR

I know it sounds illogical, but if we're in our home (or anywhere else) and feeling cold, by going outside in our bare feet, by allowing ourselves to adapt to that, when we go back inside everything is warmer. Again, we are using the cold as a force for good in our lives. In small doses like this, the cold can ignite warmth, energy and power in us. All we have to do is take off those shoes and socks and put our feet on the ground.

But not everyone will agree with me.

In some traditions, the cold is seen as an enemy to health. It's seen as a cause of sickness. I agree with that too: if we don't approach the cold with respect, and try to force our way through the experience, then the cold will show us who the boss is (and it isn't us humans). But I don't agree that the cold as a whole is bad for us. It's part of the human experience. It was there at the beginning of our lives, shocking us into breathing. So, too, is walking barefoot. Again, though, not everyone would agree. There are some people who see shoes as our saviour and think putting our feet on the bare earth is the work of the devil. I exaggerate, but you get the idea.

Again, though, if we look to nature, we usually find the answer. In my experience of raising four children, I've found that when they're young they hate putting on shoes. They find them cumbersome and restrictive. They much prefer running around in their little bare feet. My twin daughters are still fans of this – although they are developing a taste for their mother's high heels. Plus, so many martial arts are done barefoot. When our feet become strong and stable without shoes, it improves our balance, agility and stamina.

The importance of putting our bare feet on the ground really became apparent to me when I met two incredible people: Barefoot Sue and Tony Riddle. I met Sue at Prague Airport. She was barefoot and had travelled from her home in Canada to Eastern Europe (on planes, trains and automobiles) and was barefoot the whole way! Sue is an inspiring person, living life as she wants to. I loved spending time with her and watching the reactions of other people as they noticed she was walking around without shoes or socks despite the weather. Their expressions were priceless!

Tony introduced me, and countless other people, to the value of moving naturally and in bare feet. To prove its importance, Tony ran barefoot in some of the most amazing tests of endurance, such as running from one end of the UK to the other barefoot. There's plenty of science to prove the benefits of walking barefoot too.

But, most importantly, you will learn from your own experiences in the cold. Take your time. Listen to your body. Explore walking barefoot in the cold. You don't have to come visit me on the west coast of Ireland to try it (although you are very welcome to). It starts right now by taking off your shoes and socks and finding a patch of earth to stand on. By doing so, we begin to understand the cold more deeply. We begin to move a little further along the path.

Walk Barefoot

For the next three mornings, make your way out of bed, find a little patch of earth: this could be your garden, the balcony, cold concrete, your cold kitchen floor. Just find something to walk on for a few minutes barefoot. Notice how you feel when you're walking.

Notice any changes in your breathing. Notice your thoughts. We only need a little dose. Afterwards, return to your bed, or inside, and see how it feels to be back in a comfortable place again. What changes do you notice?

The
Cold Shower

Finally, they were all asleep in bed. Josie and I had tidied the house after the day's chaos. We had made all the baby bottles and lunches for the next day. Our four children were under the age of four. We had gotten through another day. It was late. It was a dark wintry night in Dublin. Josie and I slumped down on the couch. What next? Watch Netflix? I wish!

We were in the middle of a cold shower challenge. Each night, when the day's work was done, we would spend some time breathing together and then... Well, then, the most difficult part: we'd take a cold shower.

Why on earth were we doing this?

As well as having four humans to raise, having a career, and trying to have a life, we were suffering from heartache. Josie's brother, John, was an incredibly generous and supportive person. He was the type of person who helped everyone. After a tortuous battle with prostate cancer, he had died in the hospital at the end of our road. We were exhausted and stressed (like many parents) and also grief-stricken and heartbroken. If I'm being honest, we were in a bit of a hole. We needed something to get us out of it.

We had heard about the healing benefits of cold water, especially for dealing with grief and tragedy, and so had committed to having a cold shower every day. But the only time we could carve out for ourselves was last thing at night. So, there we were, sitting on the couch together, knowing that the cold shower was upstairs waiting for us.

The cold shower is probably the most convenient way of training in the cold. It's also hugely beneficial (see the section *Why Bother Getting into the Cold?* for a reminder of the benefits). Put simply, a cold shower a day can change our lives for the better.

But, like many beneficial things, it's difficult. And a bit grim.

Here's why I think it's grim: over a lifetime, many of us have grown up with deliciously hot showers. We are conditioned to see the shower and expect a warm experience. Nothing wrong with that. So, when we start cold showering, it can be a real shock to our system on every level: not only is the water cold (we'll talk more about how to deal with this in a moment) but every cell in the body expects the water to be warm. This is a new type of shock. We crave the old way. We don't like the new way. We don't want to change.

Also, our bodies know we can just step back out of the cold shower. There is a quick escape if we want to take it and that's very tempting. But, within all this shock and chaos lies the secret of the cold: it can enrich our lives. It can become a force for good.

We have to be brave though.

I'm often told by people that they hate the cold. That they despise the cold. That they can't stand the cold. Why such strong emotions?

In certain ways, the cold is like a mirror. It reflects back to us all the fear, worries, pain, discomfort and uncertainty we are holding on to; most of which we are unaware of. All of this comes rushing up to the surface when we are faced with the cold. We feel fear. We feel hatred. We feel strong resistance. All because of the temperature of the water?

My dad was a very cold person. Not emotionally; but he felt the cold a lot. For example, we were on our holidays in Spain – it was about 35°C - and my dad was still wearing a jumper and socks with his sandals. So, when he signed up for his first ice bath session, I thought to myself: 'If I can get my dad through this ice bath, I can get anyone through it.'

Dad did amazingly well in the ice bath. A week or two later, when I was visiting my parents in Portmarnock, North County Dublin, he sidled up to me and whispered: 'I'm only taking cold showers now!'

I thought, 'Wow! That's great!'

'But, dad,' I said, 'don't become a fundamentalist – we want to enjoy the hot and the cold!'

I want to be clear here (for my dad and for you): we want both hot and cold in our lives. We've evolved over millions of years to a point where, in some parts of the world, we can simply press a button and hot water flows out of the shower. Let's enjoy that. What I am suggesting, though, is that we should enjoy a nice hot shower and then at the end of it, turn it to cold. That moment of truth, of turning the tap, is the most difficult bit.

In the next chapter you will learn how to find a sense of control and calm despite the sharpness of the cold shower. You will learn how to face your fears by controlling your breath. You will learn how to see your daily hot/cold shower as a victory every time you do it. But, before we get to that, I want to ask you a question: do you really want to do it?

Let me put that another way:

Do you want to learn to conquer
your fear?
Do you want to learn to face the
difficulties in your life?
Do you want to learn to be serene
despite the pressure you face?
Do you want to feel calm and
peaceful again?
Do you want to feel powerful
every day?
Do you want to feel more alive?
Do you want to feel victorious?
Do you want to feel strong?
Do you want to feel alive?

If the answer is yes,
then it is time to turn that tap from
hot to cold.

Set Your Intention

Decide now what time of the day suits to have your cold shower. My suggestion is to incorporate it into your usual hot shower routine. Whenever you usually have a hot shower, now you do the same but finish with cold. It's important to set that intention though.

You have to commit to doing it. So, let's do that now: imagine yourself in your lovely hot shower. Imagine now, deciding it's time to turn that tap. Imagine the cold water splashing down on you. What do you do next? Let's find out.

CONTROL IN THE COLD SHOWER

Now, let's get down to business. Maybe you already take cold showers? In that case, there are ways in this chapter (and the next) for you to deepen your practice. Maybe you are unsure of how to approach the cold shower at all? In this chapter, you'll quickly begin to master that skill. We are going to learn to find a sense of control and calm in the cold, despite all the chaos. Then, all the profound benefits of the cold are ours.

Chaos

You've set your intention to do it, you're going to turn that tap to cold at the end of your hot shower.

That's done. So, what happens next? Simply put: chaos.

When the cold water hits our skin, it can feel like an explosion: it's shocking, we recoil from the water, our minds burst into fear. Usually, there is a fairly loud voice in our heads, saying 'Get the ***k out of here!'

Welcome to the chaos. This is what we want. This is where we find all the deep benefits. This is where we learn a lot about ourselves, This is where the cold teaches us. We voluntarily put ourselves into this difficult position to learn how to get out of it. It's like a battle every time we turn that tap. When it's over, we feel victorious.

For years, I used to hate this chaos. Yes, I understood it was part of the process, so I did it, but I didn't like it. Then, one day, when I wasn't feeling like myself, I decided to jump into the cold shower to change my mood. I looked at the shower and asked myself: 'Why do I hate this so much?' I thought: 'All it does is help me. Every time I get in, I feel like a better person when I get out. Every time I get in, I have more energy and my mood soars. It heals me every time.' So, from that point on, I decided to love the cold and the chaos it brings.

You may not feel that straight away, but it's an affection that will grow over time.

In the chaos, we lose track of our breathing entirely. It becomes erratic, fragmented and uneven. Our inhales become short, painful attempts at trying to breathe. Our exhalations disappear. This is where the path into the cold begins. We don't have to worry about our inhales. We'll always find a way to breathe in. Our focus is on our exhales. We want to try to find our exhales in the midst of the chaos. We want to find our exhalations, no matter how small they might be, and begin to focus on them.

Initially, our exhales will be short and choppy. They'll feel out of control.

But we must focus on them, we must begin to work on them: mechanically and consciously moving our lungs so our exhales get longer and stronger. Work them: keep focusing on them until we feel our exhales are steadily and strongly flowing outwards. It is work. The cold is relentless and will continuously try to take our breath away again. So, we have to keep working on controlling our exhales, keeping them steady, breathing out and trying to control our breath.

Let's practise it now as you read:
On your next inhale, breathe in gently and deeply.
And now, slowly and steadily, breathe all the way out.
When you reach the bottom of your exhale (without forcing it), breathe gently back in.
And now breathe slowly all the way out again.
When you reach the bottom of your breath, breathe in again.

And one last time:
Breathe calmly and steadily all the way out.
That's how we want to breathe in the cold shower.

At the beginning of the cold shower, our breathing is erratic and all over the place. That is normal. In essence, that is what we want: we want the cold to test us. We want to put ourselves into this stressful situation, so we can breathe our way out.

But, then, we want to become aware of our breathing.

Then, we want to find our exhalation in the midst of the chaos.
Then, we want to start working on that, steadily and strongly
breathing out.
Then, we want to take control of that exhale.
Then, we want to breathe out with focus and intention.

And then what?

Well, firstly (as described above), we want to find a sense
of control by breathing out steadily and strongly. That is our
focus until our breathing comes under control. Then, when
we have that sense of control, we start to slow that breath
down a little. It goes from being a little bit forceful perhaps,
to becoming a little softer. We're still focusing on that exhale.
We are still working on it. But it requires less effort now. It's
slower now.

This slowing down, this softening, then takes us deeper along the path into the cold. Then a sense of calm arises in us, despite the relentlessness of the cold. The cold water is still splashing on us, but we feel calm despite it. The cold will continue to try to take our breath away, but we are at peace in the chaos. We are in control. We are calm. Despite the chaos.

This is where the most profound benefits of the cold lie.
This is where we learn to find a sense of calm despite the chaos of the cold.
This is the path into the cold.

And why is it so important?

Well, when we can find a sense of control and calm in the chaos of the cold, we can then find it anywhere. The cold teaches us to find balance and tranquillity despite whatever pressure we are facing.

When we breathe our way into calmness in the cold, we can then do it anywhere.

For example: when a really difficult situation arises (at work or home or somewhere else), we now know we can handle it. We know because of our daily battle and victory in the cold shower that we can find a sense of calm and control by focusing on our exhale. This allows us to react differently to difficult situations. It allows us to feel differently and think differently despite the fear or worry we face. We are in control. We are calm despite the pressure.

Your mastery of the cold has begun and there is more to be done.

Exhale Calmly

Before we move further along the path into the cold, let's pause here for a moment to breathe. Our exhale is the key to finding a sense of control and calm in the cold. So, let's practise it again: as you read this, breathe in gently and now slowly and steadily breathe all the way out.

There is no forcing the breath all the way out. Let it come naturally to an end and breathe back in again. Finally, breathe calmly all the way out.

MASTERY OF THE COLD SHOWER

It seemed impossible. But we had come this far. 'We might as well try it,' I thought. Josie and I were a few weeks into our cold shower challenge. We were feeling great. Our energy had improved massively. So too had our patience with the children (and each other). We were feeling light and free. But it was late now – 10.32 p.m. – as I looked down at the piece of paper in my hand. On it was printed our cold shower challenge. Tonight's cold shower challenge was in bold: **10 minutes in the cold shower**. Those words filled me with dread. Ten minutes in there! Fear, worry, dread and everything in between swirled through my head.

Quick note: there is no need to take a 10-minute cold shower. Less is more in the cold. In the section *Listen to Your Body*, I explain in more detail how long is enough in the cold. But this was at the start of my adventures in the cold, so I thought 10 minutes was necessary. It wasn't. It was, however, an adventure into what was possible.

Josie and I made our way up the stairs quietly, trying not to wake the children. I was whispering (what I thought) were inspiring and encouraging words into Josie's ear. She had decided to go first. We crept into the bathroom and slowly closed the door behind us. Josie stepped up into the shower as my 'wise' words continued to flow. In a moment of silence, Josie turned to me and whispered through gritted teeth: 'Shut up!' She turned towards the shower, twisted the tap to cold and started breathing. It was a sight to behold: her attention was fierce; she stayed focused on keeping her breathing calm – she was ferocious in her determination. The minutes ticked by; it was so impressive.

'She's actually going to do it,' I thought. Then, another thought crept into my mind: 'Oh no, she's nearly done. Then it's my turn!'

When we're faced with a difficult task like this, we have to apply all we have learned so far: we must accept the chaos, find our breath within that and begin to focus on our exhales. Stay focused on those exhales. Feel the sense of control returning. Stay with our breathing. Slow it down a little. Gain more control of our breathing and then eventually feel the calmness arise in us. Simply put, we move from chaos to control and then to calm.

At every stage of this path, we are deriving great benefits from the cold.

When we settle into the breath, and we can find that sense of calm, then we can really begin to heal deeply. When we feel that sense of calm in the cold, our bodies have moved from fight or flight (an ancient way of dealing with danger) into a state where we can restore our health, we can replenish our energy and we can heal. Despite the pressure around us.

When we're standing in the cold shower, breathing calmly, feeling tranquil, we can go deeper again. In that moment of calm, we can let go. We can let go of whatever tension we might be holding on to. We can let go of whatever fear or stress we are clinging to. We can let go of expectations that might be overwhelming us. We can let go of all of it. We can surrender. We can leave it all behind. We let it all go as we exhale. We let go of the breath. We let go of it all.

Then, we can let go of the thing we are worried about. Then, we can release that anger and frustration. Then, we can release the grief.

Profound healing can take place in the cold. Firstly, just the experience of the cold shower and the victory of surviving it feels so beneficial. But, as we go deeper along this path and as we begin to master the experience a little more, then there are more profound benefits. It's like the body unlocks inner reservoirs of strength and resilience when we find this sense of calm in the cold. The pressure and shock of the cold is always there, but our reaction is fundamentally different when we are in this state. Despite the pressure, we can feel at peace.

How do we feel when we do this?

We feel free. We feel open. We feel light. We feel alive. We feel empowered. We have let go of whatever it is we are struggling with.

'The cold is an
opportunity to

embrace change and
grow stronger."

CONFUCIUS
CHINESE PHILOSOPHER

But, remember, this letting go in the cold is an advanced practice.

We may not get there every time. But that's alright. Sometimes, it will be a real struggle to find our breath in the cold shower. That's fine; that's what we need that day. Sometimes, we'll find our breath easily despite the cold. We'll control our exhales easily despite the cold. We'll slow them down and feel a sense of calm. We'll settle into that feeling and we'll let go of something that we've been struggling with. That's fine; that's what we need that day. Every day will be different. Every experience will be different. There is no good or bad experience. There is no 'I did a great cold shower today' nor 'I did a terrible cold shower today'. The fact that you are in there at all is spectacular. This is the practice: doing it.

The first step along this path is accepting the chaos of the cold. We get in and the chaos begins.

The path takes us deeper as we begin to control our breathing. As we focus on our exhales, they become steady and we control them.

The path takes us deeper again, as that sense of control becomes calm. Here, we feel serene and tranquil. Here, we can restore our health. Here, we can let go and feel free. And it doesn't have to be 10 minutes in the cold shower like me and Josie. You can find this power within when you turn the tap from hot to cold.

EXERCISE

Letting Go

The cold teaches us to breathe and to let go of stress and worry. But we can also do this without the cold shower: we can breathe like this whenever or wherever we need it. We can learn to let go of stress and strain now, as if we are in the cold. As you read this, breathe gently in and then slowly and steadily breathe out. Continue to breathe like this, with your focus on long, steady and calm exhales.

On your next exhale, as you breathe out, soften your shoulders. Breathe in again and as you breathe slowly and steadily out, soften your arms, hands and fingers. Breathe in again and as you breathe slowly and steadily out, soften your legs, feet and toes. This is how we breathe to let go of tension and stress. This is how we breathe in the tension of the cold.

MANTRA OF THE COLD SHOWER

So, before we go further, let's go back to the start. You're looking for something. Maybe you feel a little out of balance? Maybe you feel a bit overwhelmed? Maybe you're not feeling like yourself? You're looking for something to change that. You've heard this person and that person talk about the cold. Perhaps you've heard the sea-evangelists talking about their edifying dips in the sea? You've decided you want some of that.

You've decided to embark on the adventure of the cold shower.

You've decided to follow the path down into the cold. You've read the chapter on all the proven benefits. Yes, you want all of those. You've felt a little thrill as you stepped out of your first cold shower. You've experienced how different it made you feel.

But, you know there is more than that.

You know now that the cold can teach us in unique ways. There, standing in the cold shower, we can learn to deal with chaos and shock. There, standing in the cold shower, we can use our breathing to find a sense of control despite all the pressure and shock. There, standing in the cold shower, we can go deeper than that: we can slow those controlled breaths down and then we start to feel it: a sense of calm arises in us as we stand there and smile at the cold shower. Did you ever believe you would be able to do that?

Smile in a cold shower. Fall in love with everything in a cold shower. Soften your body, letting go of tension in a cold shower.

Did you ever think you would be able to do that?

The path into the cold teaches us all of that. Daily practice is the key though. Or, most days. Our teacher, the cold, is relentless. The cold never gives up on us. It will always be there, looking for ways to test us and our breathing, looking for a way to break our concentration. It's one of the most powerful forces of nature: the cold.

But, with daily practice, everything changes.

Yes, we will nearly always feel trepidation as we reach out to turn the shower to cold. That is natural. We want to feel that. We want to become friends with that. Then we don't fear those moments of discomfort. Instead, we become used to them. We became comfortable in that discomfort.

Our ability to find our breath in the chaos of the cold gets better. It's a skill. We become like skilful hunters, searching for our breath, finding it, holding on to it, moving the breath. Then, deepening the breath. Then, focusing on long exhales. That control of the breath allows us to slow it down. The breath begins to slow, despite the relentlessness of the cold, and then it starts to happen: a sense of calm begins to arise in us. We can settle into this, allowing the breath to slow a little more. What happens then?

The body feels safe again; it moves into the parasympathetic (peaceful) part of the nervous system. We feel tranquil; the body can adapt to the cold by generating heat and it begins to repair itself. We begin to heal.

This is advanced level training in the cold. It takes practice. It takes patience. It takes kindness to ourselves: some days we'll get there and others we won't. That is fine. That is the practice.

The act of getting into the cold and trying to control our breathing is what this is all about. There is no good or bad. There is only doing it. Being brave enough to try it. Being brave enough to do it. But, as with all skills, there is always more to learn.

The cold never stops teaching us.

I have guided thousands of people through the cold. Recently, I started to notice something new. It was happening in different places and with different people at the same time. People were discovering a new, deeper way to use the cold as a healing force and I was witnessing it.

Josie and I were jumping in and out of our ice bath one morning. I had been in already and was standing on the grass, dripping wet and smiling. Josie got into the ice bath and started the battle to find her breath. She did. I could see her find a sense of control and settle into the experience. Then, she started forcefully breathing out, repeatedly in quick succession. Again and again. It sounded powerful and looked very cathartic. Then Josie returned to soft, calm breathing before getting out.

'What was that?' I asked as she was drying off.

'I felt I had to let go of a load of tension. I was just leaving it all in the ice bath, just leaving it all there. So, I was blowing it all away. I feel great now.'

'A new way,' I thought. I filed that away in my memory.

Not long after, I was talking to a man I had been coaching for a while. He hated the cold, but had bravely followed all my guidance and had really started to feel the transformational effects of daily cold showers. I was curious and asked him to describe how he did it. He talked me through the usual battle: shock and chaos, then finding the breath, control and eventually calm. But then he said that when he felt settled into his breathing (despite the cold water), he started (what I would describe as) chanting; repeatedly saying to himself:
'I am strong, I can handle what the day brings.'
'I am strong, I can handle what the day brings.'

This chant became his long exhale. After a few rounds of chanting, he was done and he felt powerful. It reminded me of the mantras that I had repeatedly chanted in my days studying yoga. The repetition, the sound and the intention had always had a profound effect on me. Now I was seeing people doing this in the cold.

So, I practised it too. It worked. I would allow myself to get my breathing under control in the cold shower and then I would begin.

Some days, I would repeat: 'I want to let go of this stress' repeatedly in the cold. I would get out of the cold shower smiling and feeling free.

Other days, I would repeat: 'I let this water heal me.'

My mantra in the cold shower would change. But the effects were always powerful. This is an advanced practice and it's worth taking the time to explore it. I use it a lot. The people I had witnessed chanting in the cold, hadn't learned that from anyone. The cold had nudged them along the path. There is so much to learn as we follow the cold down into the depths.

Your Mantra

Imagine you're in your lovely hot shower. Turn it to cold at the end, find your breath in the chaos, slow it down and work on your breathing until you feel in control. Then, as you breathe out, start repeating your mantra (or your affirmation or your chosen phrase) to yourself over and over again. Put some energy into it. Put some feeling into it. Repeat it out loud if you can. Do this for your next three showers.

Tip: Think about what you want to say before you get into the shower. Use this exercise to let go of tension, to heal, to problem solve, to find peace, to be calm, whatever you need.

Taking
a Dip

The call ended and I stood there shocked, looking down at
the phone in my hand. 'I'd better get prepared,' I thought.
I had to be in an unexpected location in a couple of hours
with ice baths and ice and not only that: everything had to
be cleared by security before they would let me in. I had
just been asked to go to one of Ireland's oldest prisons, at
night, under the floodlights in the prison yard, and guide a
handful of prisoners through an ice bath experience. This
call came totally out of nowhere. I had never been to a
prison before. Also, I didn't know these prisoners – I had
never met them – and I only had 20 minutes to prepare
them for this incredibly difficult task. Oh, I nearly forgot to
mention, all of this was going to be recorded by a camera
crew for a TV programme.

The cold has taught me many things: one of the most
important is to surrender to what is happening, to breathe
and find a sense of calm in the chaos. So, I did; I cycled
home, got ready, packed the ice baths and drove into Dublin
city to the large green gates of the prison.

Before we get into the cold fully, immersing our body, we must be clear about why we are doing it. What is our intention? Why are we following this path? Here's my suggestion: we are learning how to use the cold as a force for good in our lives. We are learning to use it to enrich our days: making us healthier, giving us more energy, reducing inflammation, improving our immunity, and much more. How does that work in a prison?

As I stood on the ground floor of the prison, waiting to meet the prisoners, I asked myself a deeper question: what is a dip in the cold really about? I was standing in my usual shorts, T-shirt and gilet, hands behind my back, breathing softly, watching the empty stairwell in front of me. Above, soaring to the fifth floor, was landing after landing of prison cells. Somewhere above me rain dripped from a crack in the ceiling. There wasn't any trouble brewing, but the place was noisy and there was the musty smell of hundreds of men living together in cramped cells. The place had been built in Victorian times and it had an oppressive atmosphere baked into its architecture. This was a place designed to punish the humans within its walls.

There I stood, about to meet these men for the first time. Some of them would understand immediately what we were trying to do. They were looking for something more. Others would instinctively recoil from the experience. 'I hate the cold,' I heard one lad say.

'The cold is
a teacher

of resilience
and fortitude.'

LAO TZU
CHINESE PHILOSOPHER

Prison is a place of tight schedules and draconian rules. I only had a few minutes to communicate the true meaning of the experience they were going to have: it was to teach them to deal with the chaos. To teach them how to find a sense of control, despite the chaos around them in the prison or within their minds. To teach them to settle into that control, to slow down, to feel a sense of calm despite the chaos they faced. Then, they had a choice: they could decide how they wanted to react to the situation. They could decide how to feel and think about it.

That was the reason why I was standing in front of them in this oppressive place. That was why they were about to walk out onto the vast and deserted yard on a freezing night in Dublin. That was why they would strip down to their swimming shorts, and in the stark brightness of the floodlights above, step into and submerge themselves in a bath full of ice.

Once we know why we are doing this to ourselves, then we need to know how to approach the cold.

The cold must be approached with the utmost respect. It's a power we cannot fight. The cold is the boss.

The prison guards opened the first door and led us down the steps of the prison into the darkness. We were told to wait there. In a prison, I learned, there is a lot of waiting for doors to be locked and unlocked. So, as we stood on the steps, under the barbed wire, we waited until the next door could be unlocked. It was cold out here. I could see my breath as I spoke. But I needed to be clear with everyone:

'There is never any forcing or pushing in the cold,' I said. 'We are only in the cold until we have our breathing under control and then we are done. That is all we need. You are in total control of your experience in the cold. If you get in, and you don't feel it is for you today, you simply step out. If you get in and you feel an ice-cream headache coming on, you simply step out. You are in control. But, if you stay there, I will be with you, guiding you down into the depths.'

There was a silence (the first I had heard since entering the prison).

'That might work outside in the normal world,' someone shouted jokingly, 'but everyone is getting into that ice bath in here!' Everyone laughed, but I knew they understood what I had said. Some days, our time in the cold is easy. Other days, it's hard. Some days, it may not be for us at all. That's fine. (See the section *Listen to Your Body* for more on this.)

We must always respect the cold enough to listen to our bodies and know when is enough.

A shout went up from the other prison guard: the giant gates opened before us. Out there in the expanse of the prison yard, sat my two big ice baths. Watch towers loomed over us as we walked out towards the ice baths. We were about to step into the great unknown.

THE GREAT UNKNOWN

When we step into the sea, an ice bath, a cold plunge pool, a lake or river, we're stepping into the great unknown. We're not sure what awaits. We're not sure how we'll react to it. We're not sure what will happen next. It's a step into the unknown and that can be frightening (and exhilarating).

That is what it felt like as we stood around the ice baths in the prison yard. The light was strange. It was a dark night, but the prison yard lights above, the barbed wire, the watch towers and the sound of the prison behind us gave the whole thing an eerie feel.

One of the most important parts of my job is watching the body language of the people I am about to guide into the cold. Their posture, their movement, their breathing, how they are speaking, where they are looking – all of it – is like a book: it tells us a story about what is going on deep inside them. At that moment, there was a range of human reactions: some of the prisoners looked excited but in control. Others looked less so. There was one in particular that I knew would really struggle.

Before we started, we had asked ourselves what we wanted from the experience. What was our intention? I think this is one of the most important parts of preparing for a dip in the cold. It's also the thing that most people overlook. For me, I want the cold to be a force for good in my life. I want it to enrich my day. I want it to make me healthier. I want it to make me feel alive and give me energy. So, that is my intention.

Before your dip in the cold, be clear about your own intention too.

For these men, gathered around the ice baths in the prison yard (and starting to shiver in the cold night air), their intention was to learn how to be calm and in control despite the chaos they were surrounded by.

I invited the first three people to step forward and show me that they were breathing calmly before they got in. In that moment, they felt like all of us would. They felt their heart racing. Their bodies became tense as they prepared to run or fight. Their minds began to focus on the worst-case scenario. This is our in-built response to a perceived danger. All of this is to help us survive. We have evolved over millions of years to behave in this way.

But, with a bit of practice, we can learn how to transform that fear and panic. We can change those feelings into a sense of control and even calm. How? The men in the prison yard were about to find out.

Once I was satisfied that their breathing was calm enough, I shouted 'Go!' They reacted immediately, stepping over the lips of the big blue ice baths and plunging into the great unknown.

Nearly everyone reacts in the same way to a cold dip: shock and chaos. As we get into the water, we feel the chaos and the shock of the cold immediately. We might also feel pure panic, pain, confusion and everything in between. I was witnessing all of that in the ice baths in the prison yard: the struggle was underway.

But that is part of the experience. In a way, that is what we want. However, what we do next is the most important:

Firstly, we try to find our breath in the midst of all the panic. Sounds easy but the shock of the cold will shatter our senses. Our mind will be screaming 'Get out!' So, our first job is to find our breath.

Secondly, when we have found it, we start to focus on our exhales. We don't have to worry about breathing in – we'll always manage to do that. Our focus is on finding our exhales and trying to breathe out steadily; slowly trying to gain control of the exhales. The cold will relentlessly attempt to steal our breath away. So we have to stay focused on those exhales.

Finally, as we get control of our breathing, we can then slow those exhales down. When we start to control our breathing in this way, it becomes softer and calmer. We start to feel that way too: we start to feel calm despite the constant attack from the cold.

That is what I was seeing in the ice baths. In the stark light of the prison lights, I could see steam rising from the shoulders and heads of the men in the ice baths. Their breathing was steady and calm. The cold hadn't disappeared – it was there as always – but their reaction to it had changed dramatically. They were in control despite the kilograms of ice sitting on their necks, chests and shoulders. They had found calm and control in the extreme cold, under extreme pressure. Afterwards when we talked, I reminded them of the significance of that: if they can find control and calm down there in the depths of the cold, they could find it anywhere, regardless of the pressure they faced.

The cold has been proven to improve our immunity, decrease inflammation, and reduce stress, and there is even promising research showing that it may stave off dementia – see the section *Why Bother Getting into the Cold?*. If our intention is to enjoy all those benefits, then we don't need to spend lots of time in the cold: less is more. A minute or two is plenty. We don't need to time ourselves when taking a dip. Instead, we can simply listen to our breathing. It will tell us everything we need to know.

I closely watched the second group of men as they got into the ice baths. As expected, at first, their breathing was chaotic and erratic. But then, as they focused on it, they regained a sense of control. They stayed focused on their breathing and tried to slow it down.

The secret is this: if our breathing is controlled and calm, then that is how we will feel. How we breathe is how we feel and the great news is we can voluntarily change how we are breathing in every moment. By doing so, we change how we think and feel.

So, in the ice baths, the men kept working on their breath until it was under control. Then, they slowed their breathing down a little. After a few slow breaths, I saw the switch in the nervous system: it moved from stress response (sympathetic) to peace (parasympathetic). With that came a change in their demeanour: their shoulders softened, their breathing calmed, one of them even smiled at me. A sense of calm had arisen in their bodies and minds.

When we reach that point, we can settle into those feelings of control and calm. We can enjoy them. The cold will be relentlessly testing our resolve as ever. But, as ever, we stay focused on our breath. When it's controlled and calm, then our body has adapted to the pressure; it has moved into the parasympathetic (peaceful) part of the nervous system. It is adapting, it is restoring itself, it is healing. Then, we are getting all the benefits we have described. Then, the cold has become a force for good in your life. Then, it's time to get out.

Our time in the unknown is finished. We're done. We don't need to push it.

But, before we were done in the prison, there was still one more young man to go in and I knew there would be trouble.

LETTING GO IN THE DEPTHS

How did I know he would struggle? He wouldn't make eye contact when we talked. He wouldn't engage with what was going on around him. He was jumpy. His movement was erratic. His breathing was shallow and fast. He was nervous. No, I'd actually say he was terrified and that was alright. We should feel nervous and scared before doing something as difficult as getting into an ice bath on TV in prison. That energy is there to be harnessed and turned into something good. But I knew that wouldn't be the case. As the other men braved the cold and got out feeling alive and like superheroes, he recoiled.

It's a lesson for all of us: sometimes the cold isn't for us that day. It is essential that we always listen to our bodies at times like these.

I'd made it clear no one had to go in if they didn't want to. But maybe he felt pressure from the group. I'm not sure. So he edged his way towards the blue ice bath and tried to steady his breath. He stepped in and lowered himself into the freezing water. Shock and chaos streaked across his face, but he started to breathe and was really trying to find his breath. He was really trying hard to do what I had taught him. But, in the end, it was too much: the urge to fly from the situation was stronger than the desire to find a sense of calm in there. I admired his bravery for getting in at all and for attempting to stay there.

Then came the problem. When we feel agitated and panicked in the cold, we can get ourselves in trouble. In a sense, the mastery of the cold is when we get out of the water: that is when we need to stay focused and calm so our bodies can warm up naturally. If we panic, we get colder quicker and this can lead to serious problems. So I had to get his attention, and the group's, and make sure everyone stayed focused on their breathing. This kept everyone calm and focused, allowing the body to do what it does best: to adapt and in this situation warm back up.

The body makes an infinite number of calculations and adjustments to help us deal with the cold when we're taking a dip. For example, the blood vessels in our feet and fingers constrict (often painfully) to help keep our core temperature warm. This essential adjustment keeps the heart and lungs going and makes us safer despite the cold. So, the opposite is also true when we get out of the cold: our body makes a whole other set of calculations and adjustments to help us adapt to the air temperature and to stay warm.

In the prison yard, we stood and continued to breathe calmly for a minute or two before the men put their clothes back on. That gave the body time to adjust to a new temperature outside the ice bath. Everyone stayed focused on their breathing. We moved the body slowly, allowing the cold and warm blood to mix slowly and naturally. We avoided fast intense movements at this point, keeping everything slow and calm and relaxed.

Our instinct is to run around the place and put our clothes on and turn the heat up in the car straight away. But, after a dip we should, instead, stay focused on our breathing. Move slowly and slowly put our clothes back on. All of this allows the body to transition back into the warm again.

It was a profound experience out there in the prison yard under the watch towers. I admired the bravery of all the men. For a moment, I forgot where I was as we chatted. They were in disbelief. They could hardly believe that less than 30 minutes earlier they had been standing in their cells, unaware of what was about to happen. They felt proud that they were able to find the courage and strength to deal with this totally unexpected experience. A young prisoner hugged me before he left and sincerely thanked me for making the effort to come into the prison. He vowed to continue to use the cold as a way to find a sense of calm again.

As I packed the ice baths back into my car (which was in the corner of the yard), I was approached by the last prisoner, who was an older man (he reminded me of my father). He told me he felt lighter and free. He told me that he wanted to continue to practise with the cold. I told him about the cold showers. He talked of his family and how it could help them too and asked if this was my job. 'It is,' I replied. 'What a great bloody job!' he said. Our chat was short-lived as the prison guards ushered the last man away and I finished packing up.

It took a while to get back out of the prison again because of all the security checks and locking and unlocking of gates. It gave me time to think about what had just happened. It got me thinking about how the cold opens up its secrets to us the more we get into it.

These men had experienced the profound impact of the cold for the first time. But I knew, with practice, they could follow the path down into the depths of the cold. Down there, they could learn many things, including how to let go of the things they struggled with.

When we find a sense of calm and control in the cold, it feels divine. Imagine, despite the relentless attack of the cold, still being able to feel at peace. But there is more than that. We can follow the path a little deeper again. When we settle into this stillness, we can notice that our body feels tense from the cold. We can soften our body and let go of that tension.

The path goes deeper still; we can then learn to let go of the tension we hold in our minds. We can release any thoughts that have been swirling around in our heads. We can leave behind painful experiences. We can surrender to the power of the cold and let its strength work deeply on us. When we can find this calm, this stillness, and let everything else go, we can have profound experiences in the cold.

Every time I feel I have let go a little more, I realise the path goes a little deeper again. The cold never stops teaching us. When we can become calm in the cold, the path opens up to us. It doesn't matter where we are: in a prison or swimming in the sea, the path into the cold can take us deep into ourselves. When this happens, we open ourselves up to discovering new things.

EXERCISE

Calm
and Control

Your task is simple: find some cold water and sit down in it! Ideally, you want the cold water to rise up to your collar bones and not much further. This might mean filling your bath with cold water, or your local gym or recovery room might have a cold plunge pool you could use. Try the sea, a lake or a safe river. When you find your spot, ease yourself into the water. Feel the chaos and shock. Use that long exhale to bring your breathing under control.

When your breathing is under control try to slow it down a little. Once you have that sense of calm and control, settle into it for a moment and then you're done! It's not about a long time in the cold; it's about the quality of the time in there. It's about getting to a place where your breathing is calm and steady. Then you have adapted, then you are getting all the benefits.

Chapter 3

Teachings
of the Cold

Falling In Love
With Everything

Charlotte invited me to teach at her retreat in the UK. She is generous, open-hearted and full of life and uses the cold to stay balanced: 'I know it's time to go into the cold when I'm feeling overwhelmed. Or, when I feel disconnected from myself. At those times, I know I need to be brought back to the present moment. I try not to wait till I'm in total chaos before getting into the cold. I use it to stay grounded in times when I might otherwise feel out of control.'

There is a moment in the cold when everything changes. We move from chaos to calm. We move from panic to peace. We move from tension to softness. Our thoughts stop screaming 'Get out!' Instead, we are in control. We move from fear to love.

There is a moment in the cold when it feels as if we fall in love with everything. I have seen people smile at this point, despite being neck-deep in ice. I have seen people lean back and laugh, despite floating in a freezing lake. I have seen people writhe in ecstasy despite the cold. These moments don't happen every time. They might even be rare. But they do happen.

Are they important? In one sense, they are not really important. As you have already discovered, the only important thing is actually doing the work, getting into the cold and seeking the comfort in the discomfort. That is what is important. That is where all the benefits are. So actively seeking out these moments of ecstasy isn't what it's about. As with many things in life, the more we chase these experiences, the more elusive they become. So they are not the goal.

But they are part of the experience and we can learn a lot from them.

Remember, the path we are following takes us from chaos and shock in the cold down to a sense of control. All of this is done through our breathing. From there, we are simply slowing our breathing down, we are controlling it a little more. Naturally, from this slowing down, we will start to feel a sense of calm arising in us. When we keep slowing down

our breath, when we continue along the path to calmness, deeper things start to happen in us. We become calmer. We let go of tension. We let go of many of the things we have been carrying and struggling with. Down here in the depths of the cold, we can begin to heal. We can begin to restore ourselves. We can begin to find balance again.

Down here in the depths of the cold, we can see ourselves, the past, and the people in our lives more clearly. A friend of mine described it like little 'truth bombs' going off in his head.

This is mastery...

Down here in the depths of the cold, we can find answers to long-held questions, we can see clear ways out of our difficulties, we can find a new way.

Down here in the depths of the cold, we can release whatever isn't serving us anymore.

Down here in the depths of the cold, we can fall in love with everything.

We can even love the cold.

Listen
To Your Body

She was a small woman. Not very tall. But she had a strong presence and had lived a life full of adventure, love, difficulties and everything in between. Her name was Agnes and she had just died at home with us in the depths of winter.

I was startled awake by my youngest daughter standing at the doorway of my bedroom, telling me that Gaga (as Agnes was lovingly known) had died. I shook off the cobwebs of sleep and stumbled down the stairs, around to my left, through the kitchen, through the first little room and finally into Agnes' bedroom. There she lay, at peace finally, after 85 years. The rest of my family was there too.

Agnes had lived with Josie and our four children for 13 years. Agnes was my mother-in-law and I loved her dearly. We all did. The children had only ever known life with Gaga: they would sneak out into the garden and climb in the window into her room. Her room was like paradise for them. There, they would (no doubt) be treated to sweets and TV (two things we tried to limit). But that is the role of a grandparent: to layer more love and comfort onto their grandchildren.

The time after a death can be frantic, especially here in Ireland where we hold a wake and a funeral, meaning there's a great deal to organise in a very short time. Visitors came from far and wide to pay their respects, sandwiches and tea were made for all of them and much more had to be done. Once that whirlwind was over though, we all had to face what was next: heartache, grief and shock. The finality of death. The exhaustion of grief took its toll on everyone in our house. There were sore throats, coughs, chest infections, colds, headaches and blocked noses. It was emotional exhaustion.

It was a time to listen to our bodies.

Josie had nursed her mother Agnes for weeks and months before her death. She had carried Agnes and washed her and fed her towards the end. Eventually, all of that was taking its toll on Josie; she felt broken and flat.

Josie and I have an ice bath outside in the garden in a special metal shed. The ice bath used to be a big chest freezer, but had been converted into the ultimate ice bath. We called it the Vortex because getting into it was like stepping into another dimension; it is that cold. Usually, Josie and I get into the Vortex most days. It keeps us energised, healthy and full of love. 'Will you get into the Vortex with me tomorrow?' Josie asked me. 'Of course,' was my reply.

'The cold
reveals the

true strength
of character.'

ARISTOTLE
GREEK PHILOSOPHER

But, the next day, more visitors came to pay their respects to Gaga. The house was full again. There were more cups of tea and sandwiches to be made. The Vortex remained silent in the dark garden. 'I'm not sure I can get into the Vortex,' Josie said to me the following day. I knew what she meant. I felt the same.

There is a depletion that comes with raw grief that is hard to describe. But we could feel it. We listened to our bodies. The Vortex would remain silent – it would have been too much. We didn't need it that day.

As the difficult days passed, Josie changed her approach. Instead of getting into the Vortex, she finished her hot shower with a dash of cold. That was enough. The Vortex would have been too much. She listened to her body.

At the same time, the winter suddenly arrived and the air temperature plummeted. The cold was a relief in one way. It forced us to hibernate more. Josie needed time to recover; we all did. We went to bed early. We embraced the long cold evenings. We listened to our bodies.

I could feel my power returning. My body was starting to feel like itself again. My mind was still in shock, but it was clearer and ready to get back to work. When I stepped out the front door, one morning, taking the children to school, the sharp cold air brought me alive again. A couple of days before, in the depths of my exhaustion, my body had recoiled from that same cold air. I was back.

As we follow this path, listening to our bodies is an essential skill. It's something we get better at over time.

There would have been a time, years ago, when I wasn't very good at listening to my body. Instead, I was more rigid and would have forced myself into the Vortex. Some part of me would have been saying: 'You need to do this. What would people think if you weren't in the ice bath every day?' The reality is, nobody would care.

But now I respect the cold more than that. I know it can be a great force for good in our lives. I also know, as with all things, that if we push it, then it can become something different.

So, some days, you might feel like you can't take your daily dosage of cold. That is fine. Listen to your body.

Some days, you might want to try a different way of using the cold. That is fine. Listen to your body.

Some days, you might just prefer to get into a nice steaming hot bath. That is fine. Listen to your body.

Recently, I was teaching an event near Sandymount in Dublin, in a beautiful venue called the Chapel of Ease. There was a quiet builder in attendance. He was a nervous type of fella and looked at the floor a lot when talking to people. I knew from his body language that he was frightened of getting into the ice bath, which was part of the workshop. By the way, we should feel frightened before getting into the cold – it keeps us honest, respectful and focused. But, anyway, back to this fella...

He got into the ice bath eventually: he felt the shock and chaos of the cold, but he used his breathing to find control and then a sense of calm. He was delighted with himself afterwards, as he should have been – it was an incredible thing to do. Afterwards, we were having a cup of tea, and I felt he was anxious about something: he looked down at the floor and, squirming slightly, asked me: 'What will I do about wearing a work jacket? I work outside a lot, on building sites – in very windy, cold places. I usually wear a heavy work jacket. What do I do now? Can I still wear a jacket when I'm outside?'

It was a genuine question. He was confused: now that he was a conqueror of the ice bath, did he have to battle against the elements all the time? Did he have to forego all comfort now? Was it now 'cold and only cold' all the time? It all comes back to our intention: that the cold becomes a force for good in our lives. That it enriches our days. 'Enjoy your heavy work jacket,' I told him.

When we follow this path, we don't need to spend lots of time exposed to the cold. We use it in a way that helps us feel strong and whole again. We use it in a way that heals us, restores us and replenishes us.

So, if you ever find yourself, shivering, on a barren windswept building site, put your work jacket on and enjoy its warmth.

Listen to your body.

Mega-meditation

The train would come thundering by at about the same time most afternoons. The Shaolin Temple in Tufnell Park, north London, was only a few metres from the train track and only separated from it by a flimsy bamboo wall. So when that commuter train came rushing by every day, not only could we hear it, we could feel it.

I had gone to the Shaolin Temple to learn how to fight. But the Buddhist monks there first taught me how to breathe and meditate. Then, to fight.

The thundering commuter train would swing by the temple halfway through the 20-minute meditation that started our daily classes. At that stage, my hips and legs would be aching as my stiff joints got used to sitting cross-legged. The train was my way of knowing if my meditation was going well or not. Most days, I was achingly longing to hear the train; when it came I knew that my meditation was nearly over. But, on a few occasional days, I was barely aware of it at all. They were rare days.

I knew nothing about meditation then. Shifu Shi Yanzi, a calm and ferocious martial arts monk, would simply walk into the training hall and sit down on his meditation cushion, close his eyes and do – well, I'm not sure what he was doing! The rest of us would simply copy what he did: sit down and close our eyes. There was no instruction. We just had to figure it out. This went on for weeks, months and years. Eventually, I realised that there was no such thing as a good or bad meditation. The fact that we were doing it was the point.

It could be argued that the purpose of meditation is to focus on one thing (our breathing, a candle flame or something else) and by doing so, everything else falls away. By focusing on one thing, all the other worries, thoughts and activity of the mind fall away. That brings about great therapeutic benefits to the brain and body. Sounds simple, right? But, of course, it's not.

Our minds have been described as wild horses that we are desperately trying to tame. But the good news is that there's a shortcut and it comes out of your tap.

What am I having for lunch? Did I pay that bill? Will my flight be delayed?

None of these questions (or many others) come into your mind when you are submerged in the cold. In the Irish Sea, for example. For those initial moments of shock and chaos, we are consumed by the experience. There is nothing else. Our entire being is focused on survival.

The only thing we can think about is surviving the experience.

Once we get our breathing under control, that changes a little. Our mind can wander a bit but the relentlessness of the cold keeps pressing it back into survival mode.

In those moments of struggle, it's like we forget about everything else. We forget about our fears, hopes, desires and all the rest. In those moments, our mind on one level (the thinking conscious part) is fully occupied with the cold and our reaction to it. But, down below that, there is silence. Whatever patterns of thinking we usually experience are totally changed in those moments. The fabled 'monkey mind' is quiet.

Then, when we get control of our breathing and we settle down, our focus is still on the full experience. But we think about other things too. These thoughts are short-lived, though, as the cold is always reminding us that it's there: we have to stay focused to survive it. So again, the cold is teaching us, it is moulding us, it is forcing us to focus on one thing. Everything else falls away.

Welcome to mega-meditation. You don't have to spend years in silent contemplation to enjoy it; just get into the cold.

Over the years, many, many people have come to me after finding control and calm in the cold and said: 'I find meditating so difficult, I can't meditate really. But in the cold, my mind was so clear, so quiet.'

All the ways of training in the cold that you have read about so far (hands in cold water, feet on the earth, cold showers) can bring about this stillness. But this experience is particularly potent when we get neck-deep in the cold. When we just float there breathing. Or stand there in the river. Or sit there in the cold bath.

It's just us and the cold.

But there is an important difference, depending on the type of water we get into: still or wild.

Let's look at still water first. Imagine filling your bath with cold water. The water is still. Imagine going to a spa and getting into a plunge pool. The water is still (unless you put the jets on!). Imagine getting into a tub of ice. The water is still. These experiences offer us the opportunity to just sit there and fight it out with the chaos of the cold. It's an internal struggle: facing the fear, finding the breath and settling in. We can fully concentrate on the experience.

Let's take a look at wild water now. Imagine walking out into the sea. The wind is blowing; our nervous system is scanning for danger. The waves are rising and falling; our nervous system is really sensing danger. The water is rushing around us: the nervous system is telling us to get out and that's before the cold has really hit us! This is wild water and it makes the experience different.

In wild water, there are many things in our immediate environment that are demanding our attention. Our nervous system is always scanning for danger behind the scenes, especially when we are out in nature. The weather, the ground under foot, the shifting of the water and loads of other factors keep us on high alert, whether we are aware of it or not. So this adds another tantalising layer of difficulty to our experience in the cold.

Outside, in wild water, we really have to focus to find that sense of cold and control. We have to work through layer upon layer of thoughts flashing through our minds as we float on the rising sea waves. But it's possible: feel the chaos, accept it, find the breath, work on it, control it, slow it down and let the feelings of calm arise in us.

Some people really enjoy being outside in nature. Others prefer a plunge pool in a hotel. Whatever works for you.

Still or wild, the cold doesn't care. It's always there waiting for us. It's always there to teach us. It's always there to help us along the path. We don't need a Buddhist monk to show us the way; the cold is waiting to guide us.

End and
Beginning

This is the end. Well, really it's the beginning. It's the end of the book – the final chapter. But it's really the beginning of your adventure along the path. The path into the cold goes on and on. There may not be an end to it.

It's a path to empowerment, to openness, to a sense of calm and wonder.

It's a path to letting go, to finding control and calm in the chaos.

It's your path now. It's your practice. I was simply pointing the way. The work, the effort, the struggle, the victory and the joy are now all yours to experience.

We started this journey from the same place. We experienced the cold for the first time at birth. It shocked us. It traumatised us. We reacted to the cold. It brought us to life. In that moment, we were bonded to the cold (whether we liked it or not). We are now using that to our advantage.

It can make us feel alive again. It can ignite deep changes within us. It can make us whole. It can make us strong. It can make us more loving.

It starts with the chaos and shock of the cold. We find our breath and work with it until it comes under our control. Then, we slow it down. We settle into it. We feel a sense of calm arise in us. That is the way. That is the path.

It has taken me to some wonderful places. Where will it take you?

The cold comes in many forms. We can learn to use it in many ways. Sometimes putting our hands under the cold water is enough. Other times, it's repeating our mantra in the cold shower. Other times, we can simply float in the sea.

We are different every day – a little older, a little wiser perhaps – so our approach needs to be different. Whatever approach we take, we must always respect the cold. It can be healing and restorative. But it can be brutal and punishing too.

So, to help guide you along the path, I have included a map of sorts for you in this final section of the book. A path? Yes. A challenge? Yes.

It pulls together all the different exercises from the previous chapters and lays them out in sequence. You might be an experienced sea swimmer already. So for you, the path is about becoming more aware of your experience in the cold, getting more from the effort you are already making. It's about paying attention to what is happening in your body and mind in the cold. It's about finding stillness. It's about settling into a sense of calm. It's about foregoing the distraction of others, or chatting, or whatever, and coming face to face with this primal power, allowing your relationship with it to change. Will you allow it to change you? Will you let it in?

For the novice (and everyone else too), the path should be followed without force or rushing and always at your own pace. The sequence on pages 138–139 is just a suggestion. We must approach the cold with respect. We must use our common sense. We must think safety first. We must always listen to our bodies. When we do, there are great rewards and benefits to be had.

There is always more to learn. There is always more to experience in the cold.

It's the eternal teacher. It was there right at the beginning of our lives, igniting our first breath. It can become our constant companion. Our constant guide and benefactor. When we use the cold as a force for good in our lives, everything changes. All we have to do is follow the path.

Your Challenge: Follow the Path

There is always a first step. This could be yours. On pages 138–139, you will find a path down into the mysteries and benefits of the cold. It will take you gradually through all the exercises and stages described in this book.

It will get you going.

Even if you are a seasoned cold-plunger, follow the path and take your practice deeper.

I have mapped out 14 days of cold training, peaking with a full body immersion. Approach this challenge with respect for the cold (as ever). This isn't an endurance test at all. This is about your relationship with the cold changing and it becoming a force of healing, insight and restoration for you.

Each day has a specific task. Each one of those tasks is described in detail in a specific chapter of the book, so you can always go back and read through those pages again to understand the intention of each task.

This challenge is simply a signpost pointing in the direction of the cold. You can expand this challenge and change it as you see fit. You can come back to it again and again when you feel you need to reignite your cold practice. You can come back to it again when you feel you need a change in your perspective or health or mood. The cold is always there for you.

Over the next 14 days, follow the path and try the corresponding exercises, referring back to the relevant page for full details.

The most important part of this challenge is this: enjoy every step along the path! Yes, it can be hard. Yes, it can be tumultuous. Yes, there will be moments of doubt. But think about what is on the other side of all of that: freedom, openness, vitality, joy and a love for life.

Day	Task	Page
1	Cold hands: every time you wash your hands you finish with cold.	**p38–p45**
2	Cold hands: what have you noticed about your experience so far?	**p38–p45**
3	Cold hands: how do you feel before and after putting your hands in the cold?	**p38–p45**
4	Barefoot: find a patch of cold ground and see what happens.	**p46–p55**
5	Barefoot: your experience of this will be different every time.	**p46–p55**
6	Barefoot: final day of this task – what has changed for you?	**p46–p55**
7	Cold shower: control your breathing.	**p64–p70**
8	Cold shower: once your breathing is under control, can you slow it down?	**p72–p81**
9	Cold shower: when your breathing is slowed down, can you let go of the tension in your body?	**p72–p81**
10	Cold shower: mantra – this takes practise, so keep at it.	**p82–p89**

Day	Task	Page
11	Cold shower: mantra – put your passion and energy into those exhales and use the feeling of the cold to empower your affirmation or mantra.	**p82–p89**
12	Full body immersion: this could be in a cold bath, the sea, a river, a plunge pool or an ice bath - feel the shock and chaos, find your breath, focus on it, slow it down and settle into that feeling.	**p90–p111**
13	Full body immersion: try it again and find your breath and settle in. Practise this full body immersion as often as you like. There are deep benefits down there in the cold.	**p90–p111**
14	Full body immersion: This is your path now.	**p90–p111**

Index

Bibliography

Articles

pubmed.ncbi.nlm.nih.gov/17993252/

bbc.com/news/health-54531075

ncbi.nlm.nih.gov/pmc/articles/PMC5025014/

hubermanlab.com/the-science-and-use-of-cold-exposure-for-health-and-performance/

ncbi.nlm.nih.gov/pmc/articles/PMC4049052/

Books

Singer, Michael A., *The Surrender Experiment*, Yellow Kite, 2016

Dispenza, Joe, *Becoming Supernatural: How Common People Are Doing The Uncommon*, Hay House, 2017

Acknowledgements

Huge thanks to my friends and family who always support me on my adventures. Particularly my parents – Tony and Treasa – who raised me by the cold Irish Sea and nurtured my love for it. Massive thanks as well to Josie, who makes all of this possible. I love you all. I have been guided by some incredible teachers along the way and I am eternally grateful for their expertise. Finally, I acknowledge the ultimate master – the cold – it continues to teach all of us, revealing its secrets to those brave enough to get into it.

About
the Author

Níall Ó Murchú is a wellness expert with over 20 years' experience. He grew up by the Irish Sea and it was here that his curiosity for nature, and the cold, was ignited. He now teaches people all over the world how to use breathing, the cold and nature to feel calm again, to reduce stress, to improve their health, and much more. To find out more about his work, visit www.breathewithniall.com and follow him on social media @breathewithniall. If you enjoyed this book, you might also like his first best-selling book *The Blissful Breath*. Níall hosts two podcasts: Finding the Others and The Breathe With Níall Podcast. He lives in Dublin with his wife Josie, four children and Misty the cat.

Published in 2023 by Hardie Grant Books,
an imprint of Hardie Grant Publishing

Hardie Grant Books (London)
5th & 6th Floors
52–54 Southwark Street
London SE1 1UN

Hardie Grant Books (Melbourne)
Building 1, 658 Church Street
Richmond, Victoria 3121

hardiegrantbooks.com

British Library Cataloguing-in-Publication Data. A catalogue
record for this book is available from the British Library.

The Power of Cold
ISBN: 9781784886356

10 9 8 7 6 5 4 3 2 1

Publishing Director: Kajal Mistry
Commissioning Editor: Kate Burkett
Design and Art Direction: Hannah Valentine
Copyeditor: Marie Clayton
Proofreader: Caroline West
Indexer: Helen Snaith
Senior Production Controller: Sabeena Atchia

Colour reproduction by p2d
Printed and bound in China by Leo Paper Products Ltd.